Leo

Also by Sally Kirkman

SALLY KIRKMAN

Leo

The Art of Living Well and Finding
Happiness According to Your Star Sign

HODDER

First published in Great Britain in 2018 by Hodder & Stoughton
An Hachette UK company

8

Copyright © Sally Kirkman 2018

A CIP catalogue record for this title is available from the British Library

Hardback ISBN 978 1 473 67675 6

Typeset in Celeste 11.5/17 pt by Palimpsest Book Production Limited,
Falkirk, Stirlingshire

Printed in the United States of America by LSC Communications

Hodder & Stoughton policy is to use papers that are natural,
renewable and recyclable products and made from wood grown in
sustainable forests. The logging and manufacturing processes are expected
to conform to the environmental regulations of the country of origin.

Hodder & Stoughton Ltd
Carmelite House
50 Victoria Embankment
London EC4Y 0DZ

www.hodder.co.uk

Contents

• • • • •

Introduction

· · · · ·

Before computers, books or a shared language, people were fascinated by the movement of the stars and planets. They created stories and myths around them. We know that the Babylonians were one of the first people to record the zodiac, a few hundred years BC.

In ancient times, people experienced a close connection to the earth and the celestial realm. The adage 'As above, so below', that the movement of the planets and stars mirrored life on earth and human affairs, made perfect sense. Essentially, we were all one, and ancient people sought symbolic meaning in everything around them.

We are living in a very different world now, in

which scientific truth is paramount; yet many people are still seeking meaning. In a world where you have an abundance of choice, dominated by the social media culture that allows complete visibility into other people's lives, it can be hard to feel you belong or find purpose or think that the choices you are making are the right ones.

It's this calling for something more, the sense that there's a more profound truth beyond the objective and scientific, that leads people to astrology and similar disciplines that embrace a universal truth, an intuitive knowingness. Today astrology has a lot in common with spirituality, meditation, the Law of Attraction, a desire to know the cosmic order of things.

Astrology means 'language of the stars' and people today are rediscovering the usefulness of ancient wisdom. The universe is always talking to you; there are signs if you listen and the more you tune in, the more you feel guided by life. This is one of astrology's significant benefits, helping you to make sense of an increasingly unpredictable world.

Used well, astrology can guide you in making the best possible decisions in your life. It's an essential skill in your personal toolbox that enables you to navigate the ups and downs of life consciously and efficiently.

About this book

Astrology is an ancient art that helps you find meaning in the world. The majority of people to this day know their star sign, and horoscopes are growing increasingly popular in the media and online.

The modern reader understands that star signs are a helpful reference point in life. They not only offer valuable self-insight and guidance, but are indispensable when it comes to understanding other people, and living and working together in harmony.

This new and innovative pocket guide updates the ancient tradition of astrology to make it relevant and topical for today. It distils the wisdom of the star signs into an up-to-date format that's easy to read and digest, and fun and informative too. Covering a broad range of topics, it offers you insight and understanding into many different areas of your life. There are some unique sections you won't find anywhere else.

The style of the guide is geared towards you being able to maximise your strengths, so you can live well and use your knowledge of your star sign to your advantage. The more in tune you are with your zodiac sign, the higher your potential to lead a happy and fulfilled life.

The guide starts with a quick introduction to your star sign, in bullet point format. This not only reveals your star sign's ancient ruling principles, but brings astrology up-to-date, with your star sign mission, an appropriate quote for your sign and how best to describe your star sign in a tweet.

The first chapter is called 'Be True To Your Sign' and is one of the most important sections in the guide. It's a comprehensive look at all aspects of your star sign, helping define what makes you special, and explaining how the rich symbolism of your zodiac sign can reveal more about your character. For example, being born at a specific time of year and in a particular season is significant in itself.

This chapter focuses in depth on the individual attributes of your star sign in a way that's positive and uplifting. It offers a holistic view of your sign and is meant to inspire you. Within this section, you find out the reasons why your star sign traits and characteristics are unique to you.

There's a separate chapter towards the end of the guide that takes this star sign information to a new level. It's called 'Your Cosmic Gifts and Talents' and tells you what's individual about you from your star sign perspective. Most importantly, it highlights your skills and strengths, offering you clear examples of how to make the most of your natural birthright.

The guide touches on another important aspect of your star sign, in the chapters entitled 'Your Shadow Side' and 'Your Star Sign Secrets'. This reveals the potential weaknesses inherent within your star sign, and the tricks and habits you can fall into if you're not aware of them. The star sign secrets might surprise you.

There's guidance here about what you can focus on to minimise the shadow side of your star sign, and this is linked in particular to your opposite sign of the zodiac. You learn how opposing forces complement each other when you hold both ends of the spectrum, enabling them to work together.

Essentially, the art of astrology is about how to find balance in your life, to gain a sense of universal or cosmic order, so you feel in flow rather than pulled in different directions.

Other chapters in the guide provide revealing information about your love life and sex life. There are cosmic tips on how to work to your star sign strengths so you can attract and keep a fulfilling relationship, and lead a joyful sex life. There's also a guide to your love compatibility with all twelve star signs.

Career, money and prosperity is another essential section in the guide. These chapters offer you vital information on your purpose in life, and how to make the most of your potential out in the world. Your star sign skills and strengths are revealed, including what sort of job or profession suits you.

There are also helpful suggestions about what to avoid and what's not a good choice for you. There's a list of traditional careers associated with your star sign, to give you ideas about where you can excel in life if you require guidance on your future direction.

Also, there are chapters in the book on practical matters, like your health and well-being, your food and diet. These recommend the right kind of exercise for you, and how you can increase your vitality and nurture your mind, body and soul, depending on your star sign. There are individual yoga poses and tarot cards that have been carefully selected for you.

Further chapters reveal unique star sign information about your image and style. This includes whether there's a particular fashion that suits you, and how you can accentuate your look and make the most of your body.

There are even chapters that can help you decide where to go on holiday and who with, and how to decorate your home. There are some fun sections, including ideal gifts for your star sign, and ideas for films, books and music specific to your star sign.

Also, the guide has a comprehensive birthday section so you can find out which famous people share your birthday. You can discover who else is born under your star sign, people who may be your role models and whose careers or gifts you can aspire to. There are celebrity examples throughout the guide too, revealing more about the unique characteristics of your star sign.

At the end of the guide, there's a Question and Answer section, which explains the astrological terms used in the guide. It also offers answers to some general questions that often arise around astrology.

This theme is continued in a useful section entitled Additional Information. This describes the symmetry of astrology and shows you how different patterns connect the twelve star signs. If you're a beginner to astrology, this is your next stage, learning about the elements, the modes and the houses.

View this book as your blueprint, your guide to you and your future destiny. Enjoy discovering astrological revelations about you, and use this pocket guide to learn how to live well and find happiness according to your star sign.

A QUICK GUIDE TO LEO

• • • • •

Leo Birthdays: 23 July to 22 August

Zodiac Symbol: The Lion

Ruling Planet: Sun

Mode/Element: Fixed Fire

Colour: Gold, orange, colours of the sun

Part of the Body: Heart, spine and back

Day of the Week: Sunday

Top Traits: Regal, Colourful, Theatrical

Your Star Sign Mission: to create order in the world, to shine brightly and take a leading role

Best At: being the boss, playing and having fun, big-hearted generosity, stealing the show, showing off your talents, enjoying a five-star lifestyle, chasing fame and fortune

Weaknesses: bossy, self-oriented, attention-seeking, arrogant, hates being ignored, fragile ego

Key Phrase: I create

Leo Quote: 'Courage is not the absence of fear. It is acting in spite of it.' Mark Twain

How to describe Leo in a Tweet: Drama queen, larger than life persona. Takes centre stage, loves glamour & parties. Says 'stroke me, adore me, I'm a pussycat at heart'

• • • • •

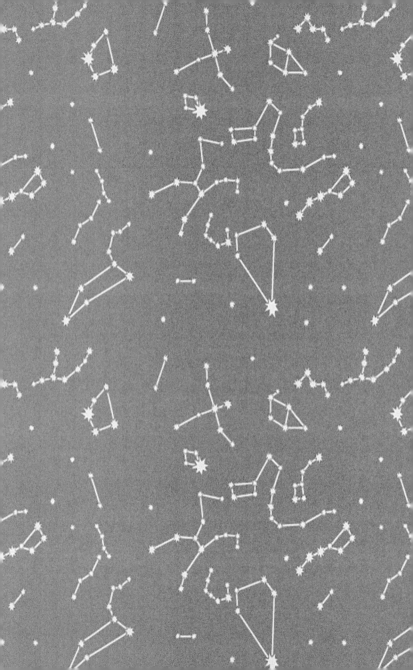

Be True To Your Sign

· · · · ·

A sunny and bright personality, warm and passionate, big-hearted and generous, loyal and courageous, the Leo character comes into the world bursting with energy and ready to be noticed.

The Sun enters your sign at the height of summer in the northern hemisphere when the temperatures heat up and the Sun's rays ripen fruit, bring flowers to full bloom and warm our bodies.

It's not surprising, therefore, that in astrology Leo is the Sun's favourite sign. The sign of Leo is where the Sun feels most at home, where it can shine brightly. In Leo, the Sun is in its sign of rulership, strong and noble.

If you love the sun and you're a sun-worshipper, then you're true to your quintessential Leo nature.

In astrology, the Sun represents vitality, energy, heat and warmth, the life force. Without the Sun to shed light on our lives, we would be in eternal darkness.

This is why your real Leo task is to find your place in the world where you too can shine brightly. When your sunny and charismatic personality is in full flow, you bring energy and dynamism into the world, and your Leo rays light up a room. Other people relax, happy to let you take charge, to be entertained, to acknowledge you as the star of the show.

The Sun is the heavenly body around which all the other planets revolve, and a typical Leo naturally gravitates towards centre stage. If you're true to your sign, you like to be in the limelight; you want to be noticed, you enjoy being the centre of attention and you love it when other people run around after you.

The Sun in astrology represents the self, the ego, and as a quintessential Leo, you are full of self-confidence and acutely aware of your self-importance. This isn't a given, however, and one of your Leo life lessons is learning to acknowledge your worth as an individual, to unlock your inner confidence, to know who you are and be proud of that person. You could say that Leo's life journey is a quest for identity.

Every Leo seeks adoration and thrives on compli-ments and praise. Without a sense of your place in the world or confirmation that other people admire you, are grateful for you or love what you do, you can lose your sense of self.

Just like the Sun, it's important that you discover how to be in some way the centre of your universe. This might mean stepping into a position of leadership or organising people or events, something you do well.

Or perhaps you prefer to take a lead role in your family, or be a teacher with an adoring audience, or find your place within your local community. One way or another, the archetypal Leo needs to find their stage on which to perform.

Being a Leo means you're a larger-than-life character who bowls through life seeking out new experiences, excitement and fun. Leo rules the fifth house in astrology, which is linked to play, games and entertainment. Add to this the fact that you're one of three extrovert fire signs along with Aries and Sagittarius, and it is no surprise that enjoyment and pleasure come high up your list of priorities.

As a Leo, it's important that you know what you love and what you're passionate about, as this is how you find fulfilment. The fifth house is related to the things we 'give birth to', including children, love affairs and creative projects. This is where you discover your skills and talents and ultimately, your personal mode of self-expression.

The quintessential Leo likes to be where the action's at and parties, events and big occasions are your stamping ground. You gravitate naturally towards group organisations and social get-togethers, often playing a chief role.

Spontaneity and fun are an integral part of your Leo personality, and you're happiest in life when you're busy and active. You rarely think twice before saying Yes to an invitation, a request or offer.

Like your zodiac symbol, the Lion, you are a natural leader, and instinctively you want to take care of others, to be proud of your tribe. Your big-hearted, generous Leo personality lends itself well to looking after others and taking charge in all kinds of ways.

In fact, it's unusual to find a Leo who thrives on their own or is continually inactive. Instead, it's through your connections with other people and your activities out in the world that your own personality flourishes. You grow in stature, your Leo heart swells and you become bigger and better because of what you accomplish.

It is rare to find a quiet, shy and retiring Leo; they do exist but, in general, your character reflects your zodiac symbol, the Lion, the most majestic of animals with a roar to match.

The lion is renowned as King of the Jungle, and this correlates with the fact that your sign of Leo is associated with royalty.

This isn't the major reason why Leo is deemed the royal sign, though. Instead, it's because of your ruling planetary body, the Sun. In many cultures throughout history, the Sun has been worshipped as a male deity, synonymous with power, strength and conscious thought. In astrology, the Sun is king of the day.

The Sun is visible to the naked eye, unlike some of the other planets, and in astrological terms, it represents sight and vision. The Sun plays a vital role in the universe and, just as it shines down on us, the classic Leo gravitates towards a superior role in life. Leo wants to be seen and noticed and will step up to rule or lead whenever the opportunity arises.

Sometimes the Leo individual creates drama for the sake of it, to be at the centre of things. Then life becomes a soap opera, with dramatic twists and turns that continually generate excitement.

At your best, you are confident and self-assured, with a healthy sense of your own importance. This isn't every Leo all of the time, however, and whether you are a loud and proud Leo lion or a timid Leo scaredy-cat depends on numerous factors.

The famous lion in *The Wizard of Oz* believed he lacked courage because he felt fear. He discovered, however, that this wasn't true because he could act bravely in the face of fear. This is real courage: being able to take action even when you feel scared.

Just because you're an enigmatic, gorgeous, vibrant Leo, who's constantly being called out to take centre stage and to step up in life, time and again, doesn't mean that you have to feel confident every minute of every day. Let your Leo light shine brightly and nurture your inner self, whatever lies behind your outer brilliance.

Your Shadow Side

One of the challenges of being a Sun Leo with a strong emphasis on the ego and self is learning how to love yourself unreservedly without coming across as a show-off or, worst-case scenario, a bossy dictator. Arrogance or a 'me, me, me' attitude is rarely engaging and usually off-putting.

This is a tricky tightrope to walk for the Leo individual. Having the Sun as your ruler means that you want and need to shine brightly, but focusing overly on your own attributes or who you are can be limiting, sometimes lonely and often disconnecting.

If the emphasis on the self is too strong, you become the embodiment of the mythological figure character Narcissus, who was known for his beauty. Narcissus was so proud he disdained those who loved him and, instead, fell in love with his own reflection. His name has become synonymous with vanity.

The fate of Narcissus was sealed when he couldn't tear himself away from his own beauty. He lost his will to live and stared at his reflection until he died. Classic stories like this are there to remind us of the pitfalls of hubris, or excessive pride; if you act in defiance of the gods, it can be your undoing. You believe you're invincible and that you have divine right, but it ultimately leads to a fall from grace.

You do have to pay close attention to the side of your Leo nature that wants to shout out to the world 'I'm brilliant; I'm amazing!' It's great for a Leo child, but in adulthood, it's important to develop a modest amount of humility so as not to become a complete show-off. Or at least choose your arena for self-promotion and ego-buffing carefully.

All signs of the zodiac can learn from their opposite, and for you that sign is Aquarius. Aquarius is about the community; it represents people and social responsibility. Aquarius is linked to humanitarian, environmental, political and collaborative goals. Aquarius considers what's best for the greater good, for the whole, rather than what's best for the individual.

Take a leaf out of Aquarius' book, and you can still shine your Leo light, but out into the world. You find your purpose, the place where you can be true to you, and your inherent qualities and gifts can benefit others.

Then, you receive love, praise and adulation in return and this is vital for the Leo archetype. If you don't feel valued or loved, your Leo light can quickly grow dim. In the wrong relationship or in a situation where your worth or esteem isn't reflected back to you, you start to fade and, in the most extreme cases, become depressed.

More than any other star sign, you desire to be acknowledged and to feel loved and you want to impress others. Where it must begin, however, is with self-love and learning to value yourself for who you are. Then you're less likely to exhibit behaviour that shouts 'love me', and instead you can stride forth in the world, confident in yourself and all that you have to offer.

Your Star Sign Secrets

Shhh, don't tell anyone but your greatest fear is that other people will recognise when you're faking it, and you'll be found out as a fraud. This happens when you don't value or trust your contribution. You believe that you have to keep proving yourself, by earning more qualifications, being better than everyone else, getting everything right all of the time. You're not an imposter; give yourself a break. This is Leo's star sign secret.

You have another secret too, around being ignored. You can be fearful that when you walk into a room, no one will notice you and you'll be invisible. This might explain why you bound through life, a stunning display of colour, vibrancy and noise. If you can't guarantee a fanfare every time you make an entrance, you'll make your own announcement in true flamboyant Leo style. Then no one can ignore you.

Your Love Life

Knowing about your star sign is an absolute essential when it comes to love and relationships. Once you understand what drives you, nurtures you and keeps you happy in love, then you can be true to who you are rather than try to be someone you're not.

Plus, once you recognise your weak points when it comes to relationships (and everyone has them), you can learn to moderate them and focus instead on boosting your strengths to find happiness in love.

> **KEY CONCEPTS:** a grand passion, a mutually appreciative love life, respect for each other, fun and fireworks, saucy sex

Cosmic Tip: Your love life will flounder big-time if you're not with a partner who worships the ground you walk on.

Being a Leo, you usually find love when you're out and about, enjoying life to the full. A typical Leo has a happy-go-lucky personality, and you like to be the life and soul of the party. Your colourful personality can attract lovers to you like a moth to a flame, and when you're in full extrovert mode, that might be all you need to get noticed.

Being the archetypal party king or queen means that you often end up in the top places, where finding a flashy or exciting lover comes naturally. Head straight for glamorous events, nightclubs and invite-only private gatherings. If you're moving in all the right circles, you'll soon find a mate, someone who you feel is deserving of you and, perhaps, who can move you up the social ladder.

If you're a classic Leo, you're not averse to social climbing and if a potential partner has famous connections, a distinguished career, they're drop-dead good-looking or ooze star quality, you're happy. You won't say no to someone who turns heads when they walk through the door, especially if it brings you closer to the spotlight.

Having a partner who makes you feel good and look good is part of the Leo package, but that's only half of it. For any relationship to last, you need to feel appreciated and ideally you want to be adored and admired as well.

If a lover's to get anywhere with you, they're wise to use compliments and flattery genuinely. You appreciate a proper courtship, and you expect the works romantically if someone's going all out to woo you. You're more interested in a grand passion than a mediocre love life.

Just as important for the Leo nature is the ability to have a laugh and a joke with your other half. Being with someone who has no sense of fun will quickly kill any spark between you.

Generosity is another key concept for you in a relationship, and you won't be happy with a partner who lacks kindness or isn't willing to help others. It's rare to find a mean Leo and, having a generous nature yourself, you expect the same in return.

If a lover can treat you royally and keep you in the manner in which you prefer to live, this is a bonus. In fact, it's something you often take into account in a relationship: how wealthy your partner is or how ambitious they are. You're not averse to being looked after, although that rarely works for you long-term.

It does have to be a case of true love, however, if you're to be willing to take on the primary wage-earner role and look after the two of you. You prefer it the other way round, with your partner being able to take care of you at least some of the time.

Relationships are essential for your Leo nature because it's through your one-to-one connections that you see yourself more clearly. In astrology, the Sun and Moon are a cosmic pair, king and queen of the day and night respectively.

The Moon shines because it reflects light from your ruler the Sun and, similarly, this is true for you as an individual. You see yourself through another person's eyes when you are in a relationship, and this is important because it both validates and reflects who you are.

In fact, if you're a typical Leo you love to be in love, and you adore being loved. Ideally, you want to be in a relationship that's a mutual adoration society, where you feel special because of the person you're with, and you know that your partner adores you.

This is vital for you if a relationship is to last past the honeymoon period. Respect for each other must be the main ingredient in a Leo relationship otherwise love can quickly lose its shine.

Once you've found your mate in life, you are one of the most loyal partners. It is important, however, that you and your other half continue to lead a life that's exciting and in the world. It's a rare Leo who wants to hide away at home with nowhere to shine or to play an influential role in life. A relationship fares best when you both have busy social lives too.

You are renowned as a drama queen or king, and sometimes you can create tension in a relationship for the sake of it. This is because you prefer life when a lot is going on, even if that means dealing with a crisis, rather than settling into a boring lifestyle.

It can make any relationship all the more exciting and if you do fall out, there's always the possibility of a chance to kiss and make up. High thrills and spills are the Leo style in love, and that's what turns you on.

For your own part, you do have to work at being good friends with your other half and not falling into the Leo trap of taking over. If you make all the decisions, it's not an equal relationship. It's also a good idea to choose your battles carefully. If you pick up on every little thing that annoys you about your other half or you become too demanding, this can push the other person away.

Rein in your ego and your need for self-validation and be appreciative of a partner who meets you halfway. This is where real happiness can be found for the loyal and loving Leo.

Finally, a relationship rarely works for you as a Leo if you aren't able to shine brightly within it. If your partner puts you down, ignores you, doesn't introduce you when you're out socially or – heaven forbid – humiliates you in public, that's a death knell for love.

Your light quickly diminishes when your partner fails to appreciate you. You often have no choice but to move on when a relationship loses its shine.

Your Love Matches

Some star signs are a better love match for you than others. The classic combinations are the other two star signs from the same element as your sign, fire; in Leo's case, Aries and Sagittarius.

It's also important to recognise that any star sign match can be a good match if you're willing to learn from each other and use astrological insight to find out more about what makes the other person tick. Here's a quick guide to your love matches with all twelve star signs:

Leo–Aries: In Your Element

Aries is a competitive sign that loves to win and come first, and your sign of Leo wants to be adored and the centre of attention. As long as you can make room for each other's egos within the relationship, this is a passionate coupling that blazes fast and furious.

Leo–Taurus: Squaring Up To Each Other

You warm each other up nicely and together you create an earthy and passionate love. You both appreciate the good things in life and are happiest when you feel comfortable in life, and preferably well off. Taurus can slip into a routine, but as a Leo, you appreciate constancy.

Leo–Gemini: Sexy Sextiles

Every day's a holiday for this combination. Life needs to be fun, and this match thrives when you put play before work. Gemini's the storyteller, and your life can be one big story or drama. The $100 question is whether Gemini can offer you the individual attention you crave.

Leo–Cancer: Next-Door Neighbours

Emotional Cancer thrives on the heat and warmth of your Leo fire. You love to be the centre of attention and lap up Cancer's caring and protective side. Treats and indulgences are a necessity, not a luxury, as this couple loves to be in pampering heaven.

Leo–Leo: Two Peas In A Pod

A loyal and loving match, two Leos is a hot combination. As long as you allow each other a turn in the spotlight, this can be a mutual adoration

41

society. You both adore fabulous parties and are generous givers of gifts. If you start a family together, children bring out your playful sides.

Leo–Virgo: Next-Door Neighbours

This love match is all about looking good and feeling good. As a Leo, you adore the attention that Virgo gives you, and prim and proper Virgo enjoys living life to the full with your fun-loving nature. If you can balance work and play, you two make a winning team.

Leo–Libra: Sexy Sextiles

This is a super-romantic match as both of you understand the importance of paying attention to your partner's needs. Anniversaries are significant, and woe betide either of you if you forget those important occasions. This combination demands a high love and romance factor at all times.

Leo–Scorpio: Squaring Up To Each Other

This is a match based on power. Leo seeks out the light whereas Scorpio searches in dark places. At your best, you can learn a great deal from each other, and if you allow each other to rule in your own way, this can be a proud and powerful pairing.

Leo–Sagittarius: In Your Element

This is a big and lively pairing as you share a mutual love of parties and living life to the full. You like to be in charge of your pride of lions, while Sagittarius is a freedom-lover and needs space. As long as you live the good life together, rather than apart, this match can not only survive but thrive.

Leo–Capricorn: Soulmates

Leo and Capricorn are made for each other. This is a power couple who want to play big in life, achieve status and make something of their lives.

It's an elegant combination, consisting of two big egos that both need a stage in life upon which to perform.

Leo–Aquarius: Opposites Attract

You are a natural extrovert who loves to perform and adores a life filled with play and a chance to be self-expressive. Aquarius is cerebral, more introverted and interested in the group and social dynamic but with a wacky side. Two unique individuals who can be best friends.

Leo–Pisces: Soulmates

Pisces and Leo is a creative combination. Leo's love of drama and Pisces's colourful imagination conjures up a magical world. Both compassionate and caring types, you enjoy the pleasure to be gained from generous and giving acts of kindness.

Your Sex Life

• • • • •

When it comes to sex, your charismatic personality can work wonders on a potential lover. You know absolutely how to turn on the charm and allure, and it doesn't often take you long to woo the one you want into your bed.

Making love is something you like to do with your particular brand of Leo style, i.e. it turns into a lavish and grand performance. You know how to make your lover feel like they are the most special person in your life – whether they are or not! – and you expect the same treatment in response.

You need sumptuous, opulent surroundings to be fully turned on. A king-sized bed and five-star luxuries are secret pleasures and the more of an effort your lover makes, the greater their reward. If someone takes you back to a dingy room with dirty sheets, it will do nothing for your libido. In fact, it could see you running for the door.

Once you've found the right location, that pleases your Leo high standards, you'll be more than happy to take proceedings to the next stage. You can be something of an exhibitionist, and a sure Leo will be happy to perform a striptease or flirt with your lover in a provocative manner. Sex is another area in which the extrovert Leo is happy to deliver.

If you're a typically passionate Leo lover, you'll do everything you can to get noticed when it comes to sex. You love the thrill of having your body explored, allowing your partner an opportunity to worship and adore you.

As long as you're not conscious of the way you look, sex with you is a passionate ride. You tend

47

to be a far better lover, however, when you stop trying to be a sex god or goddess and, instead, get in touch with your powerful sexuality.

Massaging your back is one way for your lover to turn up the heat; your back and spine can be tingling erogenous zones. Of all the senses, you relish the seductive touch most and love nothing more than the caress and feel of soft hair on your body.

Sexual pleasure is yours for the taking once you get going and, being a natural performer, you're not afraid to act out your own or your lover's fantasies. Once you recognise that lovemaking can be a truly creative act, there's no stopping you.

Your Leo fantasies often extend to making love in the sunshine, and a private picnic for two in the heat of the midday sun can trigger intense arousal and be the ideal scenario for love and frolics. Sex in the wings of a theatre or doing it in a private box at the opera also titillate the saucy Leo lover.

A five-star venue can almost guarantee good times in your book, especially if champagne is included – it's your drink of choice – and the occasion comes complete with gifts and flattery. You might even be tempted to perform for your lover while they film you, so you can both watch it back time and again.

LEO ON A FIRST DATE

- you wear your most glamorous outfit

- you expect top-quality service

- you notice whether or not your date is attentive

- you talk a lot about yourself

- you flirt outrageously

Your Friends and Family

A Leo without friends is a Leo without connection to the outside world, and that can be a sad Leo. You're one of the extrovert fire signs, and you are at your best when you find your tribe and team up with other people in life for fun, inspiration and learning.

In fact, if you're a typical Leo, you gravitate naturally towards groups of individuals for play, support and education. This is where your sign comes into its own, and you often end up in a leadership role among a group of friends.

This might mean you become team captain or committee chair. Or perhaps you unite a group of people with like minds, who come together to pursue an activity or project that's shared by and precious to all of you.

This is one of your Leo talents: being a hub for other people, knowing what your friends are yearning for, recognising what's helpful and then providing the means or the environment in which to stage an event or offer support. This is what you do well in life, and it's where Leo finds great fulfilment and satisfaction.

Being a Leo, you often want a best friend, but there's rarely just one. More likely, you have numerous friends who fill unique roles in your life, and you appreciate them all in different ways. What is essential for you when it comes to friendship is that you're noticed and appreciated for who you are.

If a friend falls out of touch and can't be bothered to contact you, it can signal the end of the friendship for the Leo character. It's a similar story if any friend shows disloyalty towards you or go out of their way to betray you. You can be quite dramatic when it comes to friendship and if someone disappoints you, that's often the end of your acquaintance.

You do expect a lot from your friends, but you also give a lot in return. You are the most generous sign of the zodiac, and you will sponsor your friend's charities, offer to join them in helping at the school fair and partner them in their projects.

You appreciate the same in return. Your best friends stand beside you in life, working towards common goals and teaming up with you to make a difference in the world.

When it comes to friendship, however, it's important to recognise that there is a side of the Leo personality that's fragile and vulnerable. A good friend must value who you are, and you'll wobble if anyone laughs at you rather than with you.

You are more susceptible to criticism than you let on. If friends point out your inadequacies rather than highlight your strengths, it can be enough to topple the Leo ego. You come across all confidence and bravado, but if someone says the wrong thing, you're prone to blushing and hate to feel humiliated.

You don't find many Leo stand-up comedians either. This is too exposing for the Leo character; you can't bear it if an audience doesn't love you. Your friendships thrive best when you appreciate each other for who you are rather than criticise for what you're not.

When it comes to family, your sign can come into its own. You want to find your tribe, your pride of lions and be a valued member of the family team. It's in your role among close family that the Leo personality often finds their place, and this can be a source of great strength for you.

However, if you can't find your place within the family and you don't feel you play a valuable role, you may choose to move away from the ones you love. Once again, it's important that you're appreciated, or you end up questioning your motives for staying involved.

The Leo parent is an adoring parent, and you want to bring out the best in your child, especially artistically and creatively. You have to be careful, however, not to allow the dominating side of your character to kick in overly but, instead, to encourage your child to be the best they can be.

When you tap into the fun-loving side of your character and the part of your personality that's still a big kid, you not only inspire children to be all that they can be but, in return, kids remind you of what's important in life.

Your Health and Well-Being

KEY CONCEPTS: healthy heart, yoga 'sun salute', an active lifestyle, Mediterranean diet, praise and encouragement

Being one of the fire signs and being ruled by the Sun is a double whammy of heat and energy. Therefore one of the principal factors for your continued good health and well-being is to stay warm. If you're a typical Leo, you won't fare well if you get too cold, and ideally you live in a location that's sunny and hot.

Failing that, escape from winter temperatures to hotter climes whenever you can. You are one of the star signs most likely to suffer from SAD – seasonal affective disorder – if you don't receive enough light in your life. This can cause you to feel sad or lethargic and, worst-case scenario, depressed.

Notice whether you're happier in sunnier weather and warmer temperatures and how it affects your mood. If it's true for you, take any necessary precautions to keep your environment warm and cosy and bright in the depths of winter. And when the sun shines, be out in it.

The parts of the body associated with your sign of Leo are the heart, the back and spine and these are the areas where to pay particular attention. Keep your heart healthy with regular exercise and don't become too sedentary.

You might be one of the livewire fire signs and burn up energy fast but Leo is a fixed sign, and not having an active lifestyle isn't right for you. This is especially important to note if you spend a lot of time sitting down for your job, for example. Then it's even more essential to factor exercise and movement into your routine.

The back and spine are the core of the body, where you find your strength. If you're prone to back pain or issues around your posture, it's essential to focus on these areas and do what you can to keep your back and spine flexible.

The yoga 'sun salute' is an ideal way of incorporating simple exercise into your routine. Traditionally, it's done at sunrise and sunset, and if you can work this into your day, even just in the summer months, it's a lovely Leo ritual. Other disciplines to look into that can benefit your posture are Pilates and the Alexander Technique; and, if you meditate, focus on the heart chakra.

The best kind of exercise for you is whatever makes you feel good. You might enjoy a hot yoga class, an energetic dance class in front of a wall of mirrors or an opportunity to learn salsa or tango, preferably in their countries of origin, i.e. somewhere hot.

Running or regular trips to the gym also suit your dynamic Leo nature. You do tend to throw yourself wholeheartedly into activities, and a healthy sense of competitive challenge can spur you on to greatness.

You might choose to train for a marathon or become a top bodybuilder, or be the best in whatever is your chosen field. You often work well with a personal trainer, someone who knows that you excel when you receive plenty of praise and encouragement.

Anything that makes your Leo personality feel special is the right kind of boost to encourage you to get fit. Find what you love and do more of it.

Factoring sufficient exercise, sleep and vitamins into your routine all helps your general well-being and gives you vital energy. Without it, you quickly become a sad cat.

The other essential ingredient in your personal Leo guide to health and well-being is happiness. This makes a huge difference to your mood and cultivating happiness in your life lifts your spirits on a daily basis.

Leo and Food

If you're typical of your sign of Leo you love the good life, and that includes food, an excessive lifestyle and indulgence.

If someone invites you to a top-class restaurant that serves Michelin-star food, you're unlikely to refuse, and you'll want the full works, aperitifs and champagne included. You have extravagant tastes, and you often have no qualms about ordering the most expensive item on the menu, especially if you're being treated to the meal.

It's a similar story if you're on a big night out. You love to have fun, and you'll be at the front of the queue ordering cocktails, and be in the thick of the action if someone suggests going on to a restaurant to eat. You gravitate towards social occasions and your ideal kind usually includes a surfeit of drinking and eating.

There may come a time in your life, if you're living 'la dolce vita' and indulging in rich food and alcohol, that you have to stop and take stock. High cholesterol is dangerous, especially for the Leo, as the heart is ruled by Leo. Regular blood pressure checks are a good idea.

The best diet for your sign is the Mediterranean diet with lashings of healthy olive oil, garlic and colourful food. In astrology foods are linked to the planetary bodies, and the Sun rules all citrus fruits in vibrant oranges, yellow and sunny colours.

The beautiful orange of saffron is a Leo spice, and fresh olives are ruled by the Sun too.

It's a good idea to limit your intake of saturated fats and instead eat healthy proteins or a vegetable-based diet. Raw food with its gorgeous rainbow colours can appeal to your Leo palate.

Vision is also connected to Leo because, in astrology, the Sun rules the right eye in a man, the left eye in a woman. This is another reason to eat a diet that's rich in leafy green vegetables, oily fish, eggs and citrus fruit, all foods that are said to benefit vision.

Do You Look Like A Leo?

There's rarely anything small or undistinctive about the Leo personality as you stride into a room with confidence. You're often on the tall side but whatever your height, you walk upright with your head held erect and a jaunty step.

Your hair is your most striking feature, and Leo women in particular have a lion's mane of hair that you can flick and swish to your heart's content. Blonde and gold flecks are classic Leo hair colours. Leo men look great bald too — a dramatic statement in itself.

There's something about the cat in many Leos, whether you have dark feline eyes or a voice that purrs. Your face is frequently oval or triangle-shaped, and you often have prominent cheek-bones and a distinctive Roman nose.

You tend to smile a lot and have great teeth. Being a sun-lover, the classic Leo has sun-kissed skin – or failing that a spray tan.

Your Style and Image

You frequently have expensive style when you're a Leo. If you have the budget to match, you will head straight for the best designers in the world to stock up on quality clothes and accessories. Coco Chanel (19 August), Yves St Laurent (1 August) and Louis Vuitton (4 August) were all born under the sign of the lion.

If you're a wealthy Leo, add Gucci, Prada and Versace to the list of chosen designers and you get an idea of your typical style. Bold and dramatic is the look, and if you're an archetypal Leo, you'll be partial to a bit of bling, flashy jewellery and designer handbags. Even if you're not loaded, that won't stop you – you'll buy fake designer goods or cheaper high-street versions of the top names' styles.

Your clothes must be eye-catching, and boots, scarves and big jackets are essential additions to the Leo wardrobe. You can pull off most styles with panache, but ultimately you look best in clothes that shout 'notice me!', statement pieces that stand out from the crowd. Suede, leather, cashmere and angora are your ideal fabrics and the typical Leo loves leopard-print.

Anything small or fussy isn't for you. Instead, you prefer to pile on the big jewellery, the accessories, the hat, the bag: the look. In fact, sometimes your style is more like dressing up, as looking striking is important to you. Add to this your love of performance and clothes become a costume, an extension of your dramatic personality.

Colour looks great on you and wearing bright-coloured clothes is good for your well-being as it makes you feel happy. Gold is the quintessential Leo colour. If you're planning a big night out, go all out to find the sparkliest, most lavish gold or glittery outfit and wow your audience. The Leo woman can dare to show off a bit of flesh, especially your back, one of the areas of the body ruled by Leo.

As a Leo, you love a chance to dress up, men included, and if you've been invited to a glamorous, star-studded event, you'll give it the works. This is where you can leap into action with a full-on beauty programme. Buffing and scrubbing, body bronzing and shimmers, and big hairstyles — think bouffant, backcombing and a tiara for the women, a ponytail for the men.

The Leo style is always dramatic and colourful and an essential part of your Leo make-up. If you can make a grand entrance and the right impression, this is a fantastic boost to your Leo confidence.

Your Home

Your Ideal Leo Home:

Leo being the regal sign, your ideal home would be a lavish palace or chateau, complete with a chauffeur-driven limousine, a banqueting hall, oodles of staff and a ballroom with a grand staircase where you can stage huge Hollywood-themed parties.

That's the fantasy anyway, although of course the

reality is that not every Leo is born into money or able to afford such luxury. That's not to say you don't have grand ideas when it comes to your home. Indeed, Leo is the sign of glamour and splendour and if your home shows off your flamboyant personality, all the better. You want the place you live in to be a show home, in some way.

If you're a typical Leo, you won't penny-pinch when it comes to furnishing your home. You like to splash your cash, and you will have at least one or two expensive items of furniture, art or ornaments that you show off with pride.

Light is a key factor in your home whether from the sun streaming in or your investing in lots of lamps or fancy lighting, as you don't like dark corners. Ideally, you'll have space to move around in, space for dancing, yoga or entertaining. The classic Leo style isn't small, delicate or dainty. Instead, you want your home to be a dramatic statement as well as a place for comfort.

You have a colourful nature, and this often shows in the colour scheme in your home. Think about the colours of the sun, and you have a good idea of the Leo palette: golds, oranges, yellows, pinks, red. You like bold colour schemes and patterns, and an iconic Leo artist is Andy Warhol (6 August).

Your taste isn't subtle, but it always grabs attention, which matters more to you. You tend to go for sumptuous and expensive fabrics, such as silk, satin, velvet and organza. Gold is your metal, so choose gold plate, brass and gilt fittings. You adore jewellery, bling and perfume and both the master bedroom and bathroom in your home will be filled with lots of beautiful accessories and beautifying products.

Your bedroom is often impressive and if you have room to put in a four-poster bed, do it. Mirrors too have pride of place in the Leo boudoir, as preening and pouting are perfect activities to boost the Leo ego. If you have room for a walk-in wardrobe, this would be an ideal addition to your home.

Unique items for the Leo home might include a cocktail bar for entertaining, an aquarium filled with goldfish, cut flowers in Leo colours and a home cinema where you can watch your favourite movies.

Overall, your ideal style is colourful and playful, dramatic yet comfortable, and even though you have expensive tastes, no one can accuse you of being precious. You tend not to worry overly about your possessions, and you will open your home up generously to other people. You prefer the place you live to be somewhere that people can gather to eat, drink, sleep, laugh and be merry.

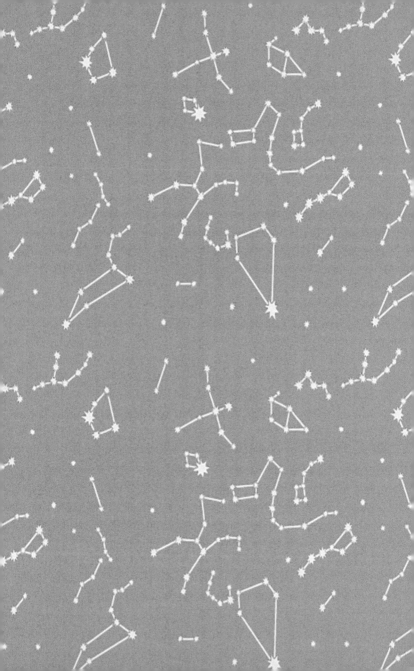

Your Star Sign Destinations

IDEAS FOR LEO:

- *a trip to Disney with kids in tow*

- *a fly–drive holiday down the Amalfi coast
  in Italy*

- *enjoy the winter sun in the Caribbean*

Did you know that many cities and countries are
ruled by a particular star sign? This is based on

when a country was founded, although sometimes, depending on their history, places have more than one star sign attributed to them.

This can help you decide where to go on holiday or take a last-minute trip away and it can also explain why there are certain places where you feel at home straight away.

You need sunshine in your life, and ideally you live in a sunny location, somewhere that gives you plenty of opportunities to take in the sun's rays. If you don't, it's essential for your Leo spirit that you head for the sun as often as you can.

This is how to boost your vitality and energy and summer holidays were made for you. Sun, sand, sea and sex — four essential ingredients for a top Leo holiday.

Your essential nature is playful and fun. Whether you head off with your family or friends, your lover or the kids, the ideal Leo holiday is a chance to let your hair down, party, relax and forget about everyday matters. Line up some summer fun every year for at least a week, if not longer. A good break from your routine is essential for you.

If you're a typical Leo, you will enjoy visiting an amusement park, a fairground, concerts in the park or a summer festival. Anywhere that gives off a holiday vibe and brings out your inner child is a great Leo mood-lifter.

You love culture too, and if you can combine sightseeing with visiting some top fashion houses, this would be the perfect Leo mini-break. Italy is one country that's both in tune with the rich and stylish side of your Leo nature and an ideal venue for romance.

The classic Leo aspires to five-star hotels and the luxury lifestyle and if you get a chance to attend any major, high-profile events around the world, grab the invitation. Whether you're hanging out at Cannes Film Festival, New York Fashion Week or the Monaco Grand Prix, you'll love cavorting alongside millionaires and billionaires, if you're not already one yourself.

You don't need a lot of money, however, to have a good time on holiday. Anywhere you can be lazy in the daytime and come out to play at nighttime will satisfy the Leo cat.

Countries ruled by Leo include Italy, Romania, the Czech Republic, the South of France

Cities ruled by Leo include Blackpool, Bath, Bristol and Portsmouth in the UK; Rome in Italy; Los Angeles, Philadelphia and Chicago in the USA; Madrid in Spain; Prague in Budapest; Mumbai in India

Your Career and Vocation

KEY CONCEPTS: a royal seal of approval, showbiz, a stage to perform on, a leadership role, ultimate responsibility

Leo is the sign of grandeur and nobility, and if your destiny involves taking on a dominant leadership role or marrying into royalty, you will do so with panache. In fact, a position in life that enables you to carry status and respect with dignity, where you're able to show off the best of your Leo character, is ideal for you.

Leo is the royal sign, and if you're born into royalty, you're in the right job. The Queen Mother (4 August), Princess Margaret (21 August) and Princess Anne (15 August) are three Leo ladies, from different generations of the UK royal family, who've played significant roles.

The new royalty is arguably celebrities. The glossy mags full of celebrity news home in on the new set of reality stars and wannabe stars, the A-listers through to the Z-listers, interspersed between photos of the young royals. This might seem an unusual career option, but the truth is there's a side to your Leo character that seeks fame and fortune. Therefore, the reality TV show can be a way in.

Many Sun Leo individuals are natural performers, and with your desire to shine, the worlds of showbiz, theatre and entertainment are ideal playgrounds for you. If you're the type of Leo who oozes confidence and you have a strong sense of yourself, you could enjoy the many perks of the celebrity world.

Done well, this can open up a lifestyle of riches and glamour. Finding an area where you can show off and express your real personality is all part of the Leo journey. You often have a natural ability to entertain others, whether on the stage or as a teacher in front of a group of kids or students. You're an excellent performer once you find your audience.

You can take your Leo skills into the world of business too, especially if you have a design or creative role. You often have a knack of coming up with new ideas that incorporate all the elements of your business but are presented in a way that's unique to you, your distinctive hallmark.

Your bright Leo personality knows how to inspire other people and get the best from them. You might work for a sales team, for example, or coach candidates who want to develop their leadership style. You are the zodiac's organiser, and your ability to see the bigger picture and to bring things together with clarity of thought makes you an indispensable member of a team.

That's not to say you always work comfortably alongside a team of people, because you tend to have strong opinions and a definite way of doing things. If you think that you can do something better than someone else on your team, it's hard for you not to point this out or even take over. A typical Leo has high standards, and you expect people who work alongside you to live up to them.

This can sometimes lead to trouble if other people accuse you of interfering or don't like the fact that you want to take charge. For your part, once you know your capabilities, you find it hard to delegate if you know you could take on a task and do it better.

Therefore, you work best as a manager or leader of people, even if you come across as being bossy.

The archetypal Leo wants to be top dog (or cat). Your direct manner instils confidence in other people, and this is important when you're responsible for a big event and a positive outcome is expected from everyone. At your best, you can take on a high-pressure role and create excellent results.

Working for yourself is another reliable option for your sign. If you believe in what you're selling and/or in your skill set, this can carry you a long way. You do however need feedback from clients or customers, more positive than negative; and ideally you'll have someone else working for you.

Administration or the detailed aspects of a job are rarely your forte, and you'd be much happier with your own PA. You thrive on work that demands a lot of you, and you're rarely satisfied in a superficial industry. Instead, you want to be in a work environment where the values of truth, honesty and confidence are honoured.

In any profession, spending too much time on your own can trigger self-doubt if you don't have some way for your value, attributes and achievements to be reflected back to you and acknowledged.

In the same way, it's important that you have sole responsibility for a task or function that belongs to you and no one else, a role in which you can shine. Whatever your chosen vocation, the Leo ego wants and needs to have ultimate control and the Leo personality loves a crown to wear.

TRADITIONAL LEO CAREERS

film star

reality TV star

entertainer

talent agent

schoolteacher

youth worker

PR specialist

events organiser

media and promotions

croupier
hotelier
gold merchant
chairperson
director
host/hostess
maître d'
poker player
speculator
business owner
prime minister

Your Money and Prosperity

If it matters to you that you can afford a luxury lifestyle, then money will obviously play a significant role in your life. Unless you're born into a privileged role, you're going to need to earn a lot of money if you want to stay in five-star hotels and lead a life of glamour.

Fortunately, the average Leo has enough drive and ambition, confidence and pizzazz to make it to the top. If you want to drink champagne all day long or you yearn for a personal chauffeur, you will need to draw up a creative work or business strategy to ensure you fly high.

Fire signs like yours make good entrepreneurs because you need a smart mix of vision and a willingness and ability to take risks if you're going to make a success of your chosen profession. Draw up a business or game plan and create a long-term grand design to keep you motivated. Focus on your skills and talents and home in on where your brand of excellence lies.

Gold is Leo's metal and is worth considering as a commodity for investment. Plus, you're the zodiac's speculator and gambler, and you shouldn't count out a win at the poker table or in the casino if you are willing to risk all. This potential fast track to prosperity will only work for the select few, but as a Leo, it is a good idea for you to explore the science behind luck, especially the Law of Attraction.

Research has shown that luck has a lot to do with strength of belief coupled with the ability to think big and take risks. The more you're attuned to what's possible in life, and you tap into the principles of abundance and unlimited thinking, the easier it becomes to unlock and increase your Leo luck factor.

If you're a typical Leo, however, you are likely to be slapdash when it comes to finances and you have to learn to be careful with money. It's a great idea to become an incessant budget-planner and list every item you purchase and every amount of money that comes in. This is a good strategy for you, because you do have an extravagant side and if you don't keep tabs on what goes where, your spending can quickly go stratospheric.

Add to this the fact that you have a hugely generous nature and you often don't think twice about treating friends and helping other people out financially. If someone needs to pick up the bill, it's invariably a Leo who steps forward. Plus, the archetypal Leo will always donate money to charity challenges, as you love to lend a hand to a good cause.

You do have to rein in your giving nature if you start to run up debt, but it's also a good strategy to practise the universal law that what you give you receive in return.

Once you take charge of your money and recognise that you are the source of your happiness and prosperity, your fortunes begin to flourish. When you truly believe you deserve the best, you can channel your confidence and self-belief into making money and being prosperous.

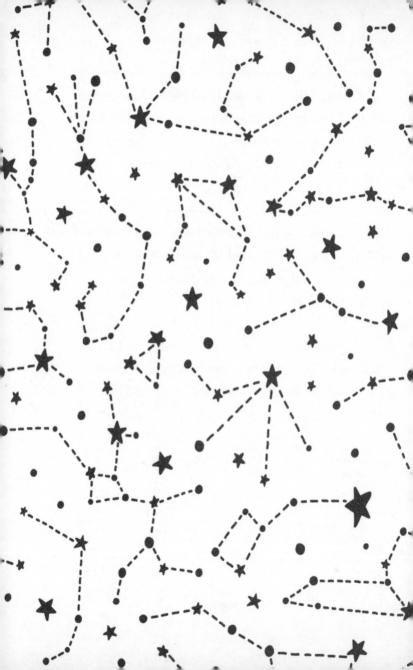

Your Cosmic Gifts and Talents

Strut Your Stuff

You are one of life's natural performers, which is why you find a myriad of Leo personalities preening their feathers and strutting their stuff on stages all around the world. Two of the most flamboyant Leo performers are Madonna (16 August) and Mick Jagger (26 July). They've been showing off their colourful Leo prowess for many years and their performances do not by any means diminish with age. So find your stage and your audience and strut your Leo stuff.

Claim Your Leo Birthright

The world needs strong rulers and if you feel drawn towards a position of responsibility or leadership, go for it. This is where Leo is at its most majestic. In astrology, your ruler, the Sun is king of the gods and, as a Leo, you are at your best when you find your subjects, the people you can teach and to whom you can impart your wisdom. Be superior, in the best possible way.

Eastenders actor Danny Dyer (24 July) found out he was a right royal geezer when he appeared on the TV programme *Who Do You Think You Are?* Although he's a cockney lad, it turns out he's a direct descendant of two kings of England and has blood ties to Henry VIII's adviser, Thomas Cromwell. Now that's a Leo story about claiming your royal birthright.

Razzle Dazzle

The world always needs more glamour, more bling, more pizzazz. Without colourful characters and displays, the world would be a drab place. This is where you can exert your Leo personality to its utmost and show the rest of us that being flamboyant, outrageous and extrovert makes life more fun. Be a loud and proud Leo, wear gold, take centre stage.

Organise An Event

As a Leo, you have the breadth of vision and the organisational skills to play big in life. In fact, your sign is brilliant at running events and being an active leader of a group of people.

Whether you're up for organising a fundraising event, a charity occasion or a community get-together, put your Leo capabilities to good use and take charge. The world always needs people to step forward to run events, and you are the perfect candidate.

Be A Hollywood Star

Hollywood is Leo's domain. Three of the four Warner brothers were Sun Leos: Albert (23 July), Sam (10 August) and Jack (2 August), plus Samuel Goldwyn (17 August) and Mr Showman himself, Cecil B. DeMille (12 August). These men were all deeply involved in the burgeoning film industry in early Hollywood, and it's testament to them that the sign of Leo remains firmly integrated into the Hollywood psyche.

As a Sun Leo, find your inner thespian, show off your star quality. You could even take yourself to Hollywood; you might just experience an epiphany and discover more about yourself on the journey.

Follow Your Heart

Leo rules the heart and you are one of the most big-hearted, generous signs of the zodiac. So trust your heart and use it to follow your instincts. Do what feels right and allow your actions to be heart-centred. This will not only bring you happiness but will benefit anyone who is a recipient of your heartfelt nature.

Follow your heart too in discovering your creative nature. When you find what motivates you and where your passion lies, magic can happen. This usually relates back to what you loved as a child and the skills and talents you enjoyed growing up. Follow your heart, find your passion and share it with other people.

15 Minutes of Fame

It was Andy Warhol (6 August) who coined the phrase 'Fifteen minutes of fame'. As a Leo, you are often motivated in life by a desire to be famous or to connect with people of influence. Use this fascination to your advantage.

Hook up with people who are already renowned, or widen your connections to meet people who can help steer your career or vocation in a positive direction. Get yourself on TV, hang out in glamorous locations and go all out to achieve your fifteen minutes of fame – as an absolute minimum.

Films, Books, Music

• • • • •

Films: *The Bodyguard* starring Whitney Houston (9 August) or *The Queen* starring Helen Mirren (26 July)

Books: The Harry Potter series by J. K. Rowling: Harry Potter shares Rowling's birthday (31 July) and Daniel Radcliffe (23 July) plays Harry Potter; *Valley of the Dolls* by Jacqueline Susann (20 August)

Music: Take your pick of Madonna's (16 August) anthems: 'Vogue', 'Holiday', 'Ray of Light', 'Material Girl'; or 'You're So Vain' by Carly Simon, backing vocals by Mick Jagger (26 July)

YOGA POSE:

Cobra: strengthens your spine and aids flexibility

TAROT CARD:

The Sun!

GIFTS TO BUY A LEO:

- amber jewellery/gold medallion
- a bunch of sunflowers
- fake tan/spray tan
- an animal onesie
- Chanel perfume
- a leopard-print coat/shoes/bag
- a fire pit or chiminea
- a home theatre system
- a limousine or helicopter ride
- Star Gift – an invitation to the Academy Awards

Leo Celebrities Born On Your Birthday

JULY

 Woody Harrelson, Fran Healy, Monica Lewinsky, Daniel Radcliffe, Alison Krauss, Slash

 Amelia Earhart, Michael Richards, Lynda Carter, Julie Graham, Jennifer Lopez, Elisabeth Moss, Anna Paquin, Danny Dyer, Jay McGuiness

25 Iman, Matt LeBlanc, Nicole Farhi

26 Stanley Kubrick, Aldous Huxley, Mick Jagger, Helen Mirren, Kevin Spacey, Sandra Bullock, Kate Beckinsale, Jason Statham, Stormzy

27 Jonathan Rhys-Meyers, Winnie Harlow, Jordan Spieth, Alex Rodriguez

28 Jacqueline Kennedy Onassis, Justin Lee Collins

29 Geddy Lee, Martina McBride, Fernando Alonso, Stephen Dorff, Joey Essex

30 Henry Ford, Emily Brontë, Henry Moore, Christopher Nolan, Arnold Schwarzenegger, Kate Bush, Laurence Fishburne, Lisa Kudrow, Vivica A. Fox, Hilary Swank

31 Wesley Snipes, J. K. Rowling

AUGUST

1 Yves Saint Laurent, Adrian Dunbar, Jerry Garcia, Coolio, Sam Mendes

2 Peter O'Toole, Alan Whicker, Wes Craven, Mary-Louise Parker, Sam Worthington

3 P.D. James, Tony Bennett, Terry Wogan, Martha Stewart, Martin Sheen, Isaiah Washington, Tom Brady, Evangeline Lilly, Jourdan Dunn, Karlie Kloss

4 Louis Vuitton, Queen Mother, Louis Armstrong, Billy Bob Thornton, Daniel Dae Kim, Barack Obama, Meghan Markle

5 Neil Armstrong, Loni Anderson, Louis Walsh, Pete Burns, Patrick Ewing

6 Alexander Fleming, Lucille Ball, Robert Mitchum, Andy Warhol, Barbara Windsor,

Geri Halliwell, Spencer Matthews, Ferne McCann, David Wolfe

7 Garrison Keillor, Mata Hari, Wayne Knight, David Duchovny, Charlize Theron, Tina O'Brien, Brit Marling

8 Betty Boop, Keith Carradine, Dustin Hoffman, The Edge, Tawny Cypress, J.C. Chasez, Roger Federer, Princess Beatrice, Shawn Mendes, Roger Hamilton

9 Melanie Griffith, Whitney Houston, Gillian Anderson, Eric Bana, Michael Kors, Audrey Tautou, Anna Kendrick

10 Kate O'Mara, Rosanna Arquette, Antonio Banderas, Kylie Jenner, Justin Theroux, June Shannon

11 Enid Blyton, Viola Davis, Hulk Hogan, Steve Wozniak, Nigel Harman, Chris Hemsworth

12 Cecil B. DeMille, Pete Sampras, Casey Affleck, Cara Delevingne

13 Alfred Hitchcock, Paul Greengrass, Phil Taylor, Marie Helvin

14 Steve Martin, Wim Wenders, Magic Johnson, Danielle Steel, Sarah Brightman, Halle Berry, Mila Kunis, Spencer Pratt

15 Napoleon, Julia Child, Princess Anne, Carol Thatcher, Alejandro González Iñárritu, Debra Messing, Ben Affleck, Jennifer Lawrence, Joe Jonas, Melinda Gates

16 T. E. Lawrence, Charles Bukowski, Ted Hughes, James Cameron, David Dickinson, Trevor McDonald, Kathie Lee Gifford, Angela Bassett, Madonna, Steve Carell

17 Samuel Goldwyn, Davy Crockett, Mae West, Robert de Niro, Larry Ellison, Belinda Carlisle, Sean Penn, Thierry Henry

18 Roman Polanski, Robert Redford, Patrick Swayze, Edward Norton, Christian Slater, Mika

19 Coco Chanel, Bill Clinton, Kyra Sedgwick, Lee Ann Womack, Matthew Perry, Lil' Romeo, Jack Canfield

20 Jacqueline Susann, Isaac Hayes, Robert Plant, Joe Pasquale, David Walliams, Fred Durst, Jamie Cullum, Kimberly Stewart, Fred Durst, Andrew Garfield, Amy Adams, Demi Lovato

21 Princess Margaret, Count Basie, Barry Norman, Kim Cattrall, Hayden Panettiere, Usain Bolt, Kelis

22 Dorothy Parker, John Lee Hooker, Honor Blackman, Tori Amos, James Corden, Kristen Wiig

23 (Gene Kelly – born on the cusp, see Q&A)

Q&A Section

• • • • •

Q. What is the difference between a Sun sign and a Star sign?

A. They are the same thing. The Sun spends one month in each of the twelve star signs every year, so if you were born on 1 January, you are a Sun Capricorn. In astronomy, the Sun is termed a star rather than a planet, which is why the two names are interchangeable. The term 'zodiac sign', too, means the same as Sun sign and Star sign and is another way of describing which one of the twelve star signs you are, e.g. Sun Capricorn.

Q. What does it mean if I'm born on the cusp?

A. Being born on the cusp means that you were born on a day when the Sun moves from one of the twelve zodiac signs into the next. However, the Sun doesn't change signs at the same time each year. Sometimes it can be a day earlier or a day later. In the celebrity birthday section of the book, names in brackets mean that this person's birthday falls into this category.

If you know your complete birth data, including the date, time and place you were born, you can find out definitively what Sun sign you are. You do this by either checking an ephemeris (a planetary table) or asking an astrologer. For example, if a baby were born on 20 January 2018, it would be Sun Capricorn if born before 03:09 GMT or Sun Aquarius if born after 03:09 GMT. A year earlier, the Sun left Capricorn a day earlier and entered Aquarius on 19 January 2017, at 21:24 GMT. Each year the time changes are slightly different.

Q. Has my sign of the zodiac changed since I was born?

A. Every now and again, the media talks about a new sign of the zodiac called Ophiuchus and about there now being thirteen signs. This means that you're unlikely to be the same Sun sign as you always thought you were.

This method is based on fixing the Sun's movement to the star constellations in the sky, and is called 'sidereal' astrology. It's used traditionally in India and other Asian countries.

The star constellations are merely namesakes for the twelve zodiac signs. In western astrology, the zodiac is divided into twelve equal parts that are in sync with the seasons. This method is called 'tropical' astrology. The star constellations and the zodiac signs aren't the same.

Astrology is based on a beautiful pattern of symmetry (see Additional Information) and it wouldn't be the same if a thirteenth sign were introduced into the pattern. So never fear, no one is going to have to say their star sign is Ophiuchus, a name nobody even knows how to pronounce!

Q. Is astrology still relevant to me if I was born in the southern hemisphere?

A. Yes, astrology is unquestionably relevant to you. Astrology's origins, however, were founded in the northern hemisphere, which is why the Spring Equinox coincides with the Sun's move into Aries, the first sign of the zodiac. In the southern hemisphere, the seasons are reversed. Babylonian, Egyptian and Greek and Roman astrology are the forebears of modern-day astrology, and all of these civilisations were located in the northern hemisphere.

• • • • •

Q. Should I read my Sun sign, Moon sign and Ascendant sign?

A. If you know your horoscope or you have drawn up an astrology wheel for the time of your birth, you will be aware that you are more than your Sun sign. The Sun is the most important star in the sky, however, because the other planets revolve around it, and your horoscope in the media is based on Sun signs. The Sun represents your essence, who you are striving to become throughout your lifetime.

The Sun, Moon and Ascendant together give you a broader impression of yourself as all three reveal further elements about your personality. If you know your Moon and Ascendant signs, you can read all three books to gain further insight into who you are. It's also a good idea to read the Sun sign book that relates to your partner, parents, children, best friends, even your boss for a better understanding of their characters too.

Q. Is astrology a mix of fate and free will?

A. Yes. Astrology is not causal, i.e. the planets don't cause things to happen in your life; instead, the two are interconnected, hence the saying 'As above, so below'. The symbolism of the planets' movements mirrors what's happening on earth and in your personal experience of life.

You can choose to sit back and let your life unfold, or you can decide the best course of action available to you. In this way, you are combining your fate and free will, and this is one of astrology's major purposes in life. A knowledge of astrology can help you live more authentically, and it offers you a fresh perspective on how best to make progress in your life.

Q. What does it mean if I don't identify with my Sun sign? Is there a reason for this?

A. The majority of people identify with their Sun sign, and it is thought that one route to fulfilment is to grow into your Sun sign. You do get the odd exception, however.

For example, a Pisces man was adamant that he wasn't at all romantic, mystical, creative or caring, all typical Pisces archetypes. It turned out he'd spent the whole of his adult life working in the oil industry and lived primarily on the sea. Neptune is one of Pisces' ruling planets and god of the sea and Pisces rules all liquids, including oil. There's the Pisces connection.

Q. What's the difference between astrology and astronomy?

A. Astrology means 'language of the stars', whereas astronomy means 'mapping of the stars'. Traditionally, they were considered one discipline, one form of study and they coexisted together for many hundreds of years. Since the dawn of the Scientific Age, however, they have split apart.

Astronomy is the scientific strand, calculating and logging the movement of the planets, whereas astrology is the interpretation of the movement of the stars. Astrology works on a symbolic and intuitive level to offer guidance and insight. It reunites you with a universal truth, a knowingness that can sometimes get lost in place of an objective, scientific truth. Both are of value.

Q. What is a cosmic marriage in astrology?

A. One of the classic indicators of a relationship that's a match made in heaven is the union of the Sun and Moon. When they fall close to each other in the same sign in the birth charts of you and your partner, this is called a cosmic marriage. In astrology, the Sun and Moon are the king and queen of the heavens; the Sun is a masculine energy, and the Moon a feminine energy. They represent the eternal cycle of day and night, yin and yang.

Q. What does the Saturn Return mean?

A. In traditional astrology, Saturn was the furthest planet from the Sun, representing boundaries and the end of the universe. Saturn is linked to karma and time, and represents authority, structure and responsibility. It takes Saturn twenty-nine to thirty years to make a complete cycle of the zodiac and return to the place where it was when you were born.

This is what people mean when they talk about their Saturn Return; it's the astrological coming of age. Turning thirty can be a soul-searching time, when you examine how far you've come in life and whether you're on the right track. It's a watershed moment, a reality check and a defining stage of adulthood. The decisions you make during your Saturn Return are crucial, whether they represent endings or new commitments. Either way, it's the start of an important stage in your life path.

Additional Information

· · · · ·

The Symmetry of Astrology

There is a beautiful symmetry to the zodiac (see horoscope wheel). There are twelve zodiac signs, which can be divided into two sets of 'introvert' and 'extrovert' signs, four elements (fire, earth, air, water), three modes (cardinal, fixed, mutable) and six pairs of opposite signs.

One of the values of astrology is in bringing opposites together, showing how they complement each other and work together and, in so doing, restore unity. The horoscope wheel represents the cyclical nature of life.

Aries (*March 21–April 19*)
Taurus (*April 20–May 20*)
Gemini (*May 21–June 20*)
Cancer (*June 21–July 22*)
Leo (*July 23–August 22*)
Virgo (*August 23–September 22*)
Libra (*September 23–October 23*)
Scorpio (*October 24–November 22*)
Sagittarius (*November 23–December 21*)
Capricorn (*December 22–January 20*)
Aquarius (*January 21–February 18*)
Pisces (*February 19–March 20*)

ELEMENTS

There are four elements in astrology and three signs allocated to each. The elements are:

fire – Aries, Leo, Sagittarius
earth – Taurus, Virgo, Capricorn
air – Gemini, Libra, Aquarius
water – Cancer, Scorpio, Pisces

What each element represents:

Fire – fire blazes bright and fire types are inspirational, motivational, adventurous and love creativity and play

Earth – earth is grounding and solid, and earth rules money, security, practicality, the physical body and slow living

Air – air is intangible and vast and air rules thinking, ideas, social interaction, debate and questioning

Water – water is deep and healing and water rules feelings, intuition, quietness, relating, giving and sharing

MODES

There are three modes in astrology and four star signs allocated to each. The modes are:

cardinal – Aries, Cancer, Libra, Capricorn
fixed – Taurus, Leo, Scorpio, Aquarius
mutable – Gemini, Virgo, Sagittarius, Pisces

What each mode represents:

Cardinal – The first group represents the leaders of the zodiac, and these signs love to initiate and take action. Some say they're controlling.

Fixed – The middle group holds fast and stands the middle ground and acts as a stable, reliable companion. Some say they're stubborn.

Mutable – The last group is more willing to go with the flow and let life drift. They're more flexible and adaptable and often dual-natured. Some say they're all over the place.

INTROVERT AND EXTROVERT SIGNS/ OPPOSITE SIGNS

The introvert signs are the earth and water signs and the extrovert signs are the fire and air signs. Both sets oppose each other across the zodiac.

The 'introvert' earth and water oppositions are:

- Taurus – • Scorpio
- Cancer – • Capricorn
- Virgo – • Pisces

The 'extrovert' air and fire oppositions are:

- Aries – • Libra
- Gemini – • Sagittarius
- Leo – • Aquarius

THE HOUSES

The houses of the astrology wheel are an additional component to Sun sign horoscopes. The symmetry that is inherent within astrology remains, as the wheel is divided into twelve equal sections, called 'houses'. Each of the twelve houses is governed by one of the twelve zodiac signs.

There is an overlap in meaning as you move round the houses. Once you know the symbolism of all the star signs, it can be fleshed out further by learning about the areas of life represented by the twelve houses.

The houses provide more specific information if you choose to have a detailed birth chart reading.

This is based not only on your day of birth, which reveals your star sign, but also your time and place of birth. Here's the complete list of the meanings of the twelve houses and the zodiac sign they are ruled by:

1 – **Aries:** self, physical body, personal goals

2 – **Taurus:** money, possessions, values

3 – **Gemini:** communication, education, siblings, local neighbourhood

4 – **Cancer:** home, family, roots, the past, ancestry

5 – **Leo:** creativity, romance, entertainment, children, luck

6 – **Virgo:** work, routine, health, service

7 – **Libra:** relationships, the 'other', enemies, contracts

8 – **Scorpio:** joint finances, other peoples' resources, all things hidden and taboo

9 – **Sagittarius:** travel, study, philosophy, legal affairs, publishing, religion

10 – **Capricorn:** career, vocation, status, reputation

11 – **Aquarius:** friends, groups, networks, social responsibilities

12 – **Pisces:** retreat, sacrifice, spirituality

A GUIDE TO LOVE MATCHES

The star signs relate to each other in different ways depending on their essential nature. It can also be helpful to know the pattern they create across the zodiac. Here's a quick guide that relates to the chapter on Love Matches:

Two Peas In A Pod – the same star sign

Opposites Attract – star signs opposite each other

Soulmates – five or seven signs apart, and a traditional 'soulmate' connection

In Your Element – four signs apart, which means you share the same element

Squaring Up To Each Other – three signs apart, which means you share the same mode

Sexy Sextiles – two signs apart, which means you're both 'introverts' or 'extroverts'

Next Door Neighbours – one sign apart, different in nature but often share close connections